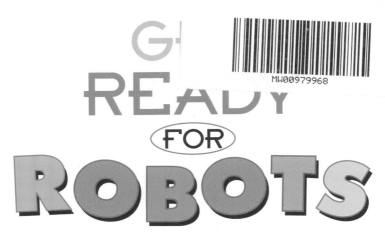

GET READY FOR ROBOTS

By Howard Gutner

Modern Curriculum Press
Parsippany, New Jersey

Photos: All photos © Pearson Learning unless otherwise noted.
Cover: Sam Ogden/Science Photo Library/Photo Researchers, Inc. Title Page:
C. Van der Lende/The Image Bank. 5: Shahn Kermani/Liaison International. 6:
Raphael Gaillarde/Liaison International. 7: Roger Ressmeyer/Corbis Corporation. 8:
Robert Giroux/Liaison International. 9: Shahn Kermani/Liaison International 10:
NASA. 11: Paul Howell/Luna Corp/Liaison International. 12: NASA. 13: Woods Hole
Oceanographic Institution. 14: Hank Morgan/S.S./Photo Researchers, Inc.
15: PhotoDisc, Inc. 16: Maximilian Stock Ltd./Science Photo Library/Photo
Researchers, Inc. 17: Ralph Garafola. 18: Hank Moran/Photo Researchers, Inc.
19: Mark Sherman/Bruce Coleman Inc. 20: Morimoto/Liaison International.
21: Liaison International. 22: Sally Corporation. 23: Photofest. 24: Volker
Steger/Science Photo Library/Photo Researchers, Inc. 25: Kaku Kurita Liaison
International. 26: Lego Mindstorms. 27: Mamoru Tsukada/Liaison International.
28: Photofest. 29: Peter Yates/Science Photo Library/Photo Researchers, Inc.
30: Sam Ogden/Science Photo Library/Photo Researchers, Inc. 31: Boeing/Liaison
International.

Cover by Lisa Ann Arcuri

Book design by Denise Ingrassia

Modern Curriculum Press
An imprint of Pearson Learning
299 Jefferson Road, P.O. Box 480
Parsippany, NJ 07054–0480

www.pearsonlearning.com

1-800-321-3106

ISBN 0-7652-1376-1

3 4 5 6 7 8 9 10 UP 08 07 06 05 04 03 02 01 00

Modern
Curriculum
Press

CONTENTS

To all the inventors of tomorrow

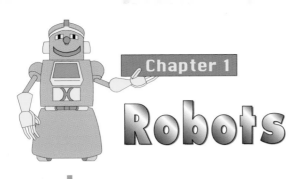

Chapter 1

Robots

Would you like to have a machine that would work for you? This machine could clean your room. It could carry things for you. It could even play games with you. A machine that could do these things is called a robot.

A housecleaning robot ▶

Directing a robot with a remote control

A robot is a machine that can be told what to do. Then the robot can do a job by itself. It will do the job over and over again until a person tells it to stop.

A computer is inside almost all robots. The computer can be programmed. This means that people tell the computer what they want the robot to do. Then the computer controls every move the robot makes.

Building a robot ⬇

➤ **Mark Tilden, a robot scientist, makes robots that look like insects.**

Robots come in many shapes and sizes. Some robots are just an arm and a hand. Others look like boxes on wheels. Some robots are shaped like animals. Others look a little bit like people.

Robots do many different things. They mow lawns. They help to build cars. They carry big boxes. They go to the bottom of the sea. Robots have even been in movies.

A robot housecleaner ▶

Robot Fact

Some robots walk and talk. Some even feel hot and cold. No robot can feel happy or sad as people do.

Chapter 2

Robots Explore

Robots do things that are too hard for people to do. They also go places where it is not safe for people to go. One of these places is outer space.

A robot spacecraft flies by the planet Jupiter.

A robot works on the moon.

It takes a long time to travel from Earth to planets like Mars or Venus. People are not yet able to make these long trips. Robots have no problem going into space. They do not need to sleep. They do not need food. They do not even need air to breathe!

↟ The robot *Sojourner* on Mars

In 1997 a spacecraft called *Pathfinder* landed on Mars. A little robot named *Sojourner* came out of the spacecraft. Scientists on Earth told *Sojourner* where to go. They told it to look at dirt and rocks. *Sojourner* also took lots of pictures. The pictures helped the scientists find out what Mars is like.

Robots also go to the bottom of the sea where it is too deep for people to go. The robots take pictures of plants and animals. They look at the soil.

Robots can also find things under the sea. A robot named Jason Junior helped find the *Titanic*. This was a big ship that sank many years ago. Jason took pictures inside and outside of the ship.

Jason Junior about to enter the *Titanic* ⬇

People cannot walk into volcanoes. The heat and poison gases would kill them. In 1994, a robot named Dante II went into an active volcano.

Dante II walked down into the volcano crater. It studied the gases. It also made a map of the volcano.

Dante II

Robot Fact

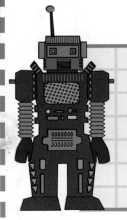

Many robots collect information. Then people are needed to tell what the information means.

Chapter 3

Robots at Work

Each robot is made to do one kind of job. Some robots work in factories. They do jobs that people don't want to do. People might find these jobs tiring or boring. Robots never get tired or bored. They can also do some jobs better and faster than people.

▼ **A factory robot**

Many robots work in car factories. Some robots run carts that carry car parts. The carts go to other robots who make the cars. The car robots are really just big arms that put the car bodies together.

▼ Robot arms make cars.

Some robots paint the cars. This job is dangerous for people to do. The smell of the paint can make people sick. The smell doesn't bother the robots.

Robot arm painting a car

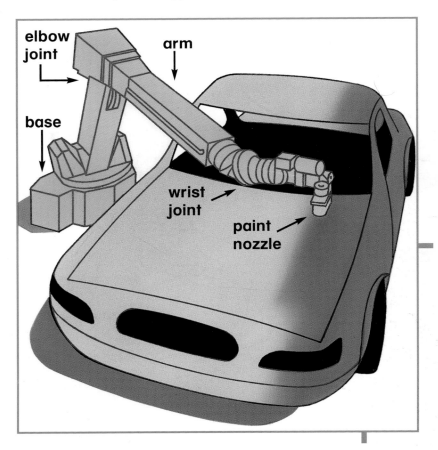

elbow
joint

arm

base

wrist
joint

paint
nozzle

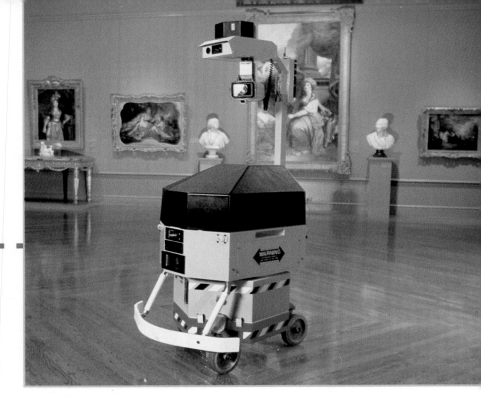

A guard robot on duty in a museum

Many robots work as guards. This is good work for robots. Unlike people, robots do not fall asleep! They can be on guard all day and all night.

Some of these robots have good memories. They know if a chair or a desk has been moved. They can hear footsteps. They can even smell smoke.

In Japan some robots are used to direct traffic. They direct cars around places where a road is being fixed. The highway workers are glad they don't have to do that job. Sometimes cars hit the robots by accident.

Robot directing traffic

▲ **A robot checks gas tanks.**

Another robot in Japan checks big gas tanks for leaks. The robot climbs down the tank like a spider. The robot rarely falls even when the wind blows. The gas from any leaks the robot finds also won't hurt it.

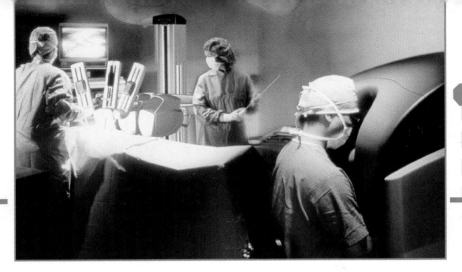

▲ **A robot helps doctors during a heart operation.**

Robots also help doctors. One kind of robot is used when a person needs a hip bone fixed. Another kind of robot helps a doctor work on a person's heart.

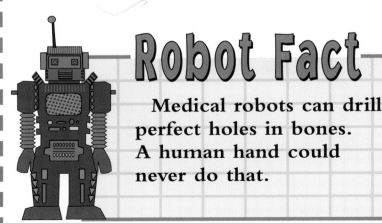

Robot Fact

Medical robots can drill perfect holes in bones. A human hand could never do that.

Chapter 4

Fun With Robots

Robots are machines. They can't have fun like people do. Yet robots help people have fun all the time. Robots sing and even dance at some fairs and parks.

Robots play music.

A dinosaur in the movie *Jurassic Park* ▶

Robots are also in movies. A few years ago a movie was made about dinosaurs. It was called *Jurassic Park.* The movie dinosaurs looked very real. Many of them were robots. They moved and even roared. They gave people a good idea of how real dinosaurs may have looked and moved.

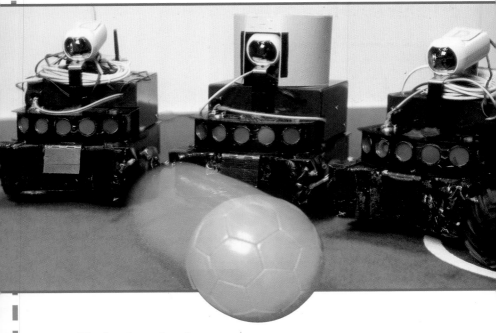

 Robots playing soccer

Robots can also play sports. *RoboCup* is a soccer game for robots. It is played once a year. Scientists from all over the world enter the robots they have built.

The robots play on teams. People tell the robots what to do. Then the robots move the ball across the field.

There is a robot that can play volleyball. The robot has cameras in its head. The cameras find the ball by its color. Then the robot can pick up and hit the ball. The robot can also sense where the ball will go next.

Robot playing volleyball

Toy robots are fun. The newest robot toys have small computer chips in them. A person can give the toy an order. Then it will walk and even speak.

Robot toy

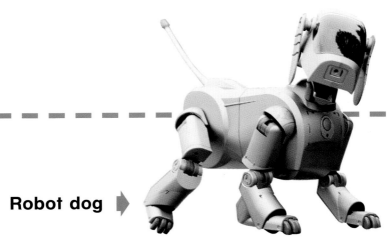

Robot dog ▶

There are even robot pets. A robot dog named Aibo will bark and walk. It will chase a ball and wave hello. Aibo acts happy when it wags its tail and flashes its eyes. Most people think the robot dog is fun, but not as much fun as a real dog.

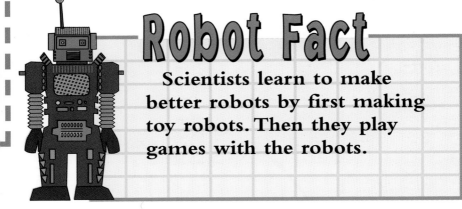

Robot Fact

Scientists learn to make better robots by first making toy robots. Then they play games with the robots.

Chapter 5

Robots in the Future

What will robots be like in the future? Some scientists think robots will become more like people. It will be many years though before robots can think and act like people.

C-3PO and R2-D2 from the movie *Star Wars* ⬇

A robot leading a blind person ▶

Robots in the future will help more people. Scientists are now working on a robot that can lead blind people. The blind person holds the robot like a cane. The robot leads the person. It goes around anything that is in the way.

Scientists are also working on making robots that can understand what they see and hear. Robots today can't tell if they are looking at a tree or a stop sign. They can't tell if they are hearing a dog bark or a car horn.

This robot named Cog learns like a human baby does. ➡

▲ **A robot plane like this one may go to Mars one day.**

Better robots are also being made to go into space. Scientists are working on a robot plane to send to Mars. The plane will take close-up pictures.

Robots will soon be able to do many things they can't do now. What would you like your future robot to do?

Robot Fact

Today some robots can learn from their mistakes. The next step is to make robots that can think before they act.

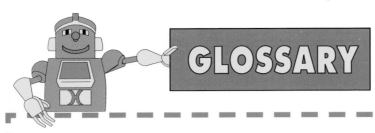

GLOSSARY

accident   [AK sih dunt] something that happens that is not planned

computer   [kum PYOO tur] a machine that stores and works with facts

drill   [drihl] make a hole with a special tool

factories   [FAK tuh reez] places where things are made

machine   [muh SHEEN] an object with moving parts that does work

scientists   [SYE un tihsts] people who work in and know about science

sense   [sens] to become aware of

volcano   [vahl KAY noh] a mountain from which comes hot, liquid rock and ash